CAT SQUARE MOSAICS COLORING BOOK

COLORFUL ANIMALS COLLECTION

PUBLISHED IN 2018 BY
KODOMO PUBLISHING

COPYRIGHT 'ILLUSTRATIONS' 2018 KODOMO PUBLISHING
ALL RIGHT RESERVED. 'NO PART OF THIS PUBLICATION MAY BE REPORDICED OR TRANSMITTED IN ANY
FORM OR BY ANY MEANS. ELECTRONIC, OR MECHANICAL,INCLUDING PHOTOCOPY, RECORDING OR ANY
INFORMATION STORAGE SYSTEM AND RETRIEVAL SYSTEM WITHOUT PERMISSION IN WRITING BY
PUBLISHER 'KODOMO PUBLISHING'

PRINTED IN THE UNITED STATES OF AMERICA

COLOR PALETTE

0	White
1	Yellow
2	Light Orange
3	Dark Orange
4	Cream
5	Red
6	Dark Red
7	Pink
8	Violet
9	Dark Pink
10	Dark Purple
11	Light Blue
12	Sky Blue
13	Medium Blue
14	Dark Blue
15	Yellow Green
16	Medium Green
17	Bright Green
18	Dark Green
19	Tan
20	Light Brown
21	Dark Brown
22	Light Gray
23	Dark Gray
24	Black

COLOR TEST PAGE

1
2
3
4
5
6
7
8
9
10
11
12

13
14
15
16
17
18
19
20
21
22
23
24